# Garfield rolls On

BY: JIM DAVIS

BALLANTINE BOOKS · NEW YORK

All rights reserved under International and Pan-American Copyright Conventions. Published in the United States by Ballantine Books, a division of Random House, Inc., New York, and simultaneously in Canada by Random House of Canada Limited, Toronto.

Library of Congress Catalog Card Number: 85-90570

ISBN: 0-345-32634-2

Manufactured in the United States of America

First Edition: October 1985

10 9 8 7 6 5 4 3 2 1

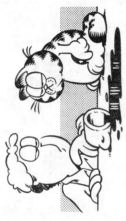

© 1984 United Feature Syndicate, Inc.

© 1984 United Feature Syndicate, Inc.

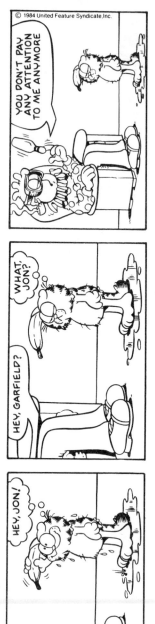

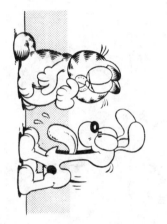

WELL, WELL, WELL. I SEE YOU'RE EATING MY FOOD, ODIE. NOW WHAT ARE WE GOING TO DO WITH YOU?

WE ARE GOING TO KICK YOU INTO NEXT WEEK! THAT'S WHAT WE'RE GOING TO DO!

PUNT

LUNCH ISN'T THE SAME WITHOUT ODIE. HE ALWAYS SLIPS UP BEHIND ME, BARKS LOUDLY AND MAKES ME FALL INTO MY FOOD

© 1984 United Feature Syndicate, Inc.

I GUESS I'LL JUST HAVE TO MAKE DO

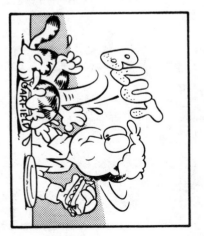

BLURT

© 1984 United Feature Syndicate, Inc.

WHERE'S ODIE?

SOMEWHERE OVER SATURDAY

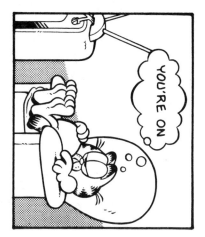

SURF'S UP!

STAND ASIDE THERE, FELLA. HERE COMES MY NEXT WAVE

B-2

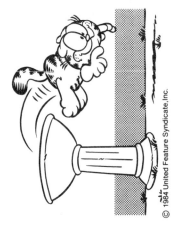

© 1984 United Feature Syndicate, Inc.

BUT YOU LOOK RIDICULOUS

GREAT!

B-1

JIM DAVIS

GARFIELD, I KNOW YOU LIKE TO HAVE FUN...

© 1984 United Feature Syndicate, Inc.

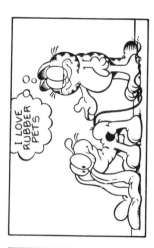

AS LONG AS IT ISN'T IN DARK SCARY PLACES

8-22

JIM DAVIS

THE CAPED AVENGER FORGOT TO CORRECT FOR CROSSWIND

BLAT!

THE CAPED AVENGER SEEKS OUT EVIL WHEREVER IT MAY LURK

THE CAPED AVENGER WILL NOW DESCEND UPON AN OLD ARCHENEMY

8-25

JIM DAVIS

GUESS WHAT, GARFIELD! WE'RE GOING TO THE FARM THIS WEEK

WHOOPTY-DOO. GOING TO THE FARM IS LIKE GOING TO THE ZOO...

WHERE THEY EAT EVERYTHING BUT THE CATS

DAD! MOM!

JONNY! JON BOY!

I WISH THEY'D CALL ME BY MY REAL NAME

YOU'RE RIGHT, DUMMY

© 1984 United Feature Syndicate, Inc.

© 1984 United Feature Syndicate, Inc.

WELL, GARFIELD, THIS WEEK YOU LEARNED WHERE BACON COMES FROM

BACON COMES FROM A PIG

DO YOU KNOW WHAT WORRIES ME, GARFIELD?

JPM DAV9S 9-1

AND YOU LEARNED WHERE MILK COMES FROM

MILK COMES FROM THE UDDER OF A COW

MY GRANDFATHER WAS BALD, MY DAD IS BALD AND MY BROTHER IS BALDING

NOT TO WORRY

WOULD YOU LIKE TO KNOW WHERE EGGS COME FROM?

I WOULD AS SOON THAT REMAIN A MYSTERY

8-31

JPM DAV9S

YOU ARE PROBABLY ADOPTED

OKAY, GUYS,
GET ON YOUR MARK,
GET SET, GO!

HERE, STRETCH,
HAVE AN APPLE.

COMPETITION IS APPARENTLY
NOT A DRIVING FORCE IN
THEIR LIVES

STOMP!

FOO!

DONG!

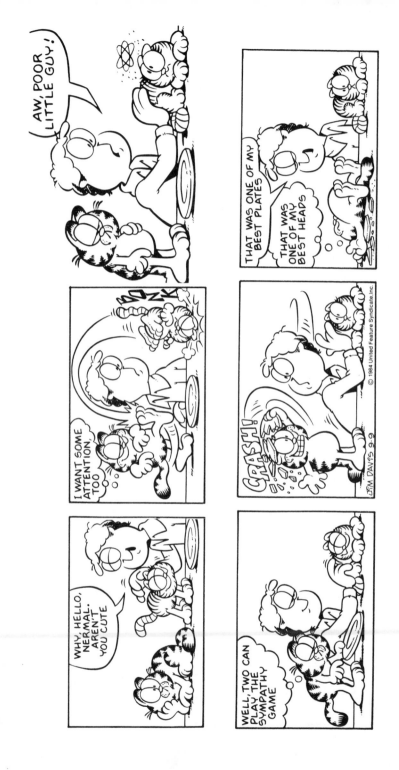

READY FOR A GOURMET MEAL, GARFIELD?

I LOVE YOUR PURR, GARFIELD

PURRR

WHAM!

I WISH THERE WERE A WAY TO GET THE PURR WITHOUT THE CAT

PURRR

I HATE SPIDERS

BUT I GUESS YOU HAVE TO TAKE THE BAD WITH THE GOOD

YOU'RE TREADING ON THIN ICE, FELLA

HEE HEE. THERE'S MORE THAN ONE WAY TO SKIN A CAT

RATS. GARFIELD FELL ASLEEP IN THE MIDDLE OF THE FLOOR

9-15

WHIRRRR!

HAVE YOU EVER TRIED TO PICK UP A SLEEPING CAT?

HOW PROPHETIC

IT'S IMPOSSIBLE

IN ORDER TO PROPERLY DIET, YOU MUST CHANGE YOUR EATING HABITS, GARFIELD

JIM DAVIS

9-18

© 1984 United Feature Syndicate, Inc.

YOU MUST LOOK AT FOOD DIFFERENTLY

HA HA HA, GARFIELD

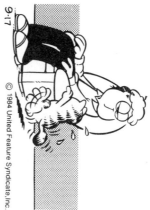

9-17

© 1984 United Feature Syndicate, Inc.

IT'S DIET TIME, GARFIELD

I WAS AFRAID OF THAT

JIM DAVIS

FOR ONCE IN MY LIFE, A DIET WORKED

9-21

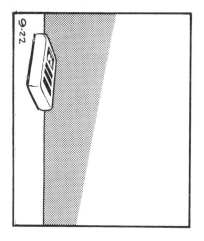

9-22

I'M GOING TO TREAT MYSELF TO A POTATO CHIP

© 1984 United Feature Syndicate, Inc.

LET'S SEE HOW I DID ON MY DIET THIS WEEK

RATS

POOMP!

WHIMPER

OH, SHUT UP

© 1984 United Feature Syndicate, Inc.

I THOUGHT FAT PEOPLE WERE JOLLY

JIM DAVIS

9-30

© 1984 United Feature Syndicate, Inc.

© 1984 United Feature Syndicate, Inc.

GOOD NIGHT, GARFIELD

I THINK I'LL TRY A TWO-AND-A-HALF NAP ATTACK IN THE PIKE POSITION WITH A HALF TWIST

10-6

© 1984 United Feature Syndicate, Inc.

DON'T LET THE THING IN THE CLOSET GET YOU

CLICK

DON'T DO THAT TO ME!

© 1984 United Feature Syndicate, Inc.

I'LL SETTLE FOR A BELLY-FLOP

POOMP!

GOOD MORNING, FOLKS! MY, OH MY, IT'S A BEAUTIFUL MONDAY MORNING OUT THERE

JIM DAVIS

10-15

© 1984 United Feature Syndicate, Inc.

OUR SATELLITE PICTURE SHOWS CLOUDS OVER THE NORTHEAST, SUNNY SKIES IN THE SOUTHWEST...

10-16

OUR WEATHER RADAR SHOWS CLEAR SKIES WITH NO RAIN IN SIGHT

TRAFFIC BACKED UP ON 12TH STREET

© 1984 United Feature Syndicate, Inc.

EXCEPT OVER ONE HOUSE IN THE SUBURBS

AND MY LITTLE NIECE, SALLY, PLAYING IN HER SANDBOX IN TEXAS

KIND OF SCARY, ISN'T IT?

JIM DAVIS

HERE COMES ARLENE. SHE'S CRAZY ABOUT ME

JIM DAVIS

DO YOU LOVE ME MORE THAN YOU LOVE FOOD, GARFIELD?

GARFIELD 10-23

HEY, ARLENE, WHAT'S MY MOST OUTSTANDING FEATURE?

YOU'RE FAT

10-22

DO CHICKENS HAVE LIPS?

GARFIELD

JIM DAVIS

DID YOU HEAR THAT? SHE ADMIRES ME FOR MY BODY

NO

BINGO

GARFIELD

© 1984 United Feature Syndicate, Inc.

© 1984 United Feature Syndicate, Inc.

© 1984 United Feature Syndicate,Inc.

GOOD MORNING, MOUSE

GOOD MORNING, CAT

JIM DAVIS

© 1984 United Feature Syndicate, Inc.

GARFIELD, THERE'S A MOUSE IN THE HOUSE, AND I'M JUST SICK ABOUT IT

JIM DAVIS

10-29

MAKE YOURSELF AT HOME

GLADLY

10-30

IT CHEWED THE TOE OUT OF MY SOCK

BUT FIRST, SOME HOUSE RULES

I WANT YOU TO CATCH IT AND KILL IT

NOW I'M SICK ABOUT IT

© 1984 United Feature Syndicate, Inc.

GARFIELD! COME HERE!

"GARFIELD" THIS, "GARFIELD" THAT. I'M SICK OF MY NAME

HEY, FLEABAG! COME HERE!

THEN AGAIN,"GARFIELD" DOES HAVE A CERTAIN RING TO IT

OH, NO! A FLEA! I'M GETTING YOU A FLEA COLLAR, GARFIELD

LET'S NOT BE TOO HASTY HERE

LOOK AT THOSE DISTINCTIVE YELLOW AND GREEN MARKINGS THERE

THIS FLEA IS A MEMBER OF A RARE SPECIES OF VEGETARIANS

JIM DAVIS

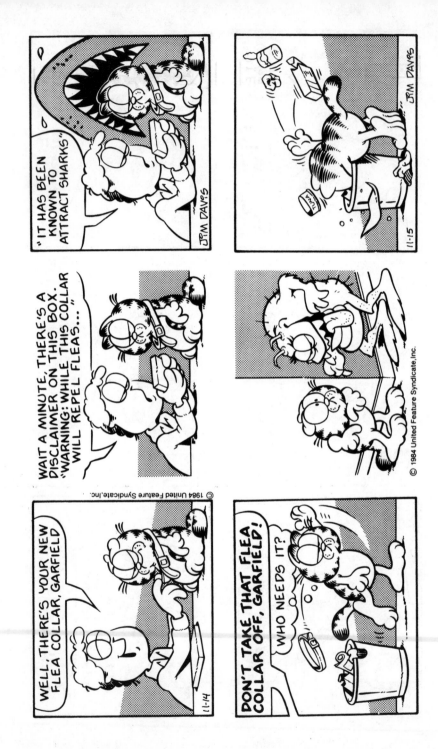

YOU HAVE A PRETTY GRIM FLEA PROBLEM THERE, ODIE

THAT'S NOT A VERY STRONG FLEA COLLAR

JIM DAVIS 11-16

DID I EVER TELL YOU ABOUT MY CRAZY UNCLE BERLE? HE THOUGHT HE WAS A DOG

JIM DAVIS 11-17

THE POOR GUY WAS ALWAYS EXHAUSTED

HE KEPT CHASING HIMSELF UP TREES

OH, BY THE WAY, DOC BOY, I'VE FIXED US UP ON A DOUBLE DATE

HEY, GREAT!

JPM DAVPS 11-23

© 1984 United Feature Syndicate, Inc.

DOC BOY! OUR DATES ARE HERE!

© 1984 United Feature Syndicate, Inc.

WHAT'S A DOUBLE DATE?

THAT'S WHEN YOU AND I GO ON A DATE TOGETHER

EEEEEEK!

GEE, IT SEEMS LIKE IT WOULD BE MORE FUN IF SOME GIRLS CAME ALONG

THERE'S NO HOPE

CAN WE TALK?

CAN WE LAUGH?

JPM DAVPS 11-24

GARFIELD, I'M GOING TO A CARTOONISTS' CONVENTION, AND THE MOTEL WHERE I'M STAYING WON'T ACCEPT PETS

I'M LEAVING FOR THE CARTOONISTS' CONVENTION NOW, GARFIELD. THERE'S A WEEK'S WORTH OF FOOD FOR YOU

A WEEK'S WORTH, HUH?

SORRY, ODIE, YOU CAN'T GO

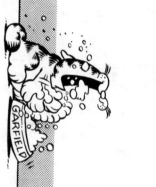

GARFIELD, YOU ARE A PET

RATS! I KEEP FORGETTING

SNAP!

IT WAS MORE LIKE 11 SECONDS' WORTH

© 1984 United Feature Syndicate, Inc.

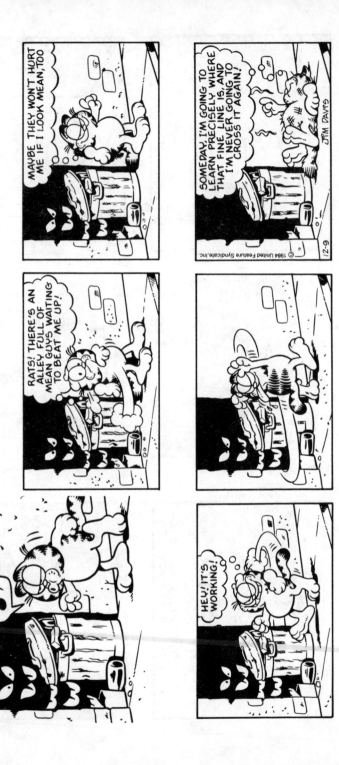

GEE, I MISS HAVING GARFIELD AROUND. I EVEN MISS THE ABUSE

JIM DAVIS 12·17

I'D LOVE TO CATCH YOUR MICE, GRANDPA, BUT I HAVEN'T SEEN ANY WORTHY OF MY TIME. GOT ANYTHING BIGGER?

BRING ON THE TRAINING MOUSE!

JIM DAVIS 12·18

© 1984 United Feature Syndicate, Inc.

RRR!

© 1984 United Feature Syndicate, Inc.

ME AND MY BIG MOUTH

THANKS, ODIE, BUT IT JUST ISN'T THE SAME

© 1984 United Feature Syndicate, Inc.

# TO THE PROSPECTIVE CARTOONIST

Al Capp once said, "You must have two qualities to be a successful cartoonist. First, it helps to have been dropped on your head as a small child. Second, you must have no desire, talent, or ability to do anything useful in life."

While his may seem a somewhat flippant observation, it nevertheless reflects how seriously cartoonists take themselves and their art. If I had only one piece of advice to give a prospective cartoonist, it would be:

HAVE FUN WITH YOUR FEATURE!

If you have fun doing it, people have fun reading it. Your enthusiasm comes through.

Most hopeful cartoonists labor their creations. An overworked, heavily laden cartoon strip or panel doesn't have the charm or witty appeal of a simply drawn, simply stated sentiment. All a cartoonist has to do is hold a mirror to life and show it back with a humorous twist. More often than not, when a reader laughs at a strip, it's not because it's funny, but because it's true.

PREPARE YOURSELF...

HERE ARE SOME GENERAL RECOMMENDATIONS TO LAY THE GROUNDWORK FOR A CAREER IN CARTOONING...

1) GET A GOOD LIBERAL ARTS EDUCATION. Enroll in journalism courses, as well as art classes. DO A LOT OF READING. The better read you are, the more natural depth your writing will have. Learn to draw realistically. It helps any cartooning style.

2) SEEK AN ART OR JOURNALISM RELATED JOB. This affords you the luxury of having food to eat until you make a go of it in cartooning.

3) EXPERIMENT WITH ALL KINDS OF ART EQUIPMENT AND MATERIALS. I use India ink and a #2 Windsor-Newton sable brush. For lettering, I use a Speedball B-6 point. I work on Strathmore 3-ply bristol board, smooth surface.

4) **STAY MOTIVATED.** Try to get your work published in a school paper, local newspaper or local publication. Many cartoonists give up the quest a year or two before they would have become marketable.

5) **PREPARE NEAT, THOUGHTFUL SUBMISSIONS TO THE SYNDICATE EDITORS.** Send only your best work and be prepared to submit it many times. I could wallpaper a bedroom with *my* rejection slips.

Again, don't forget to keep it simple and have fun. Oh, yes...a little luck along the way never hurts.

JIM DAVIS

GOOD LUCK!